The Art of Good Food

PASTA SAUCES

The Art of Good Food

PASTA
SAUCES

JON HIGGINS

Illustrated by

PAUL COLLICUTT

CHARTWELL
BOOKS, INC.

The Art of Good Food

Pasta Sauces

Designed and created by

THE BRIDGEWATER BOOK COMPANY LTD

Designer Sarah Stanley

Editor Donna Wood

Managing Editor Anna Clarkson

Illustrations Paul Collicutt

Page makeup Lee Forster

CHARTWELL BOOKS

A division of Book Sales, Inc.

POST OFFICE BOX 7100

114 Northfield Avenue

Edison, N.J. 08837

CLB 4572

© 1996 COLOUR LIBRARY BOOKS LTD

Godalming, Surrey, U.K.

All rights reserved.

Color separation by Sussex Repro, England

Printed and bound in Singapore by Tien Wah Press

ISBN 0-7858-0375-0

Contents

Introduction

Pasta in all its various shapes and sizes is a good friend of even the most inexperienced cook. Whether you are using fresh or dried varieties the addition of a few well-chosen ingredients to the cooked pasta can make a tasty and satisfying meal.

If there is one golden rule to working with pasta it would have to be to use the freshest ingredients possible – the freshest herbs, the freshest cheeses, the freshest oils. This is important because often the sauces are cooked only very briefly, sometimes not at all, so the freshness benefits not only the taste but the appearance, too.

WHAT TYPE OF PASTA SHOULD I USE?

Part of the fun of cooking with pasta is that you can use whatever type you fancy. Perhaps a red tagliatelle or a black spaghetti, maybe some fresh penne or dried orecchiette?. The choice is entirely yours, the only difference being the amount of cooking time required. (Dried pasta takes approximately twice as long to cook as fresh.)

WHICH IS BETTER, FRESH OR DRIED?

It is a common misconception that dried pasta is a poor relation to fresh varieties. This is not the case. There are many excellent dried pastas available that are capable of producing better results than some fresh ones.

SO HOW DO I TELL LINGUINE FROM FUSILLI, FROM CONCHIGLIE?

A good question! There is a seemingly endless number of pastas available, and every time you go to buy some, there will be another type new to the shelves to make choosing even more difficult. Fortunately, retailers are realizing this and labeling the packages much more clearly, even giving English names to those variations with tongue-twister titles. This may upset the pasta purists but it will give the rest of us the confidence we need to try them.

I NEVER SEEM TO COOK THE RIGHT AMOUNT OF PASTA!

The majority of recipes contained in this book allow 4 ounces of pasta per person, a good average figure on which to base your requirements. Of course you can serve pasta as a starter if you wish, in which case 2 ounces per person should suffice.

A FEW TIPS ON COOKING PASTA

1. Use the saucepan one size up from that originally chosen. Pasta needs plenty of room to cook, otherwise it may stick together.

2. Add a few drops of oil to the cooking water as well as plenty of salt; this will also help prevent the pasta from sticking.

3. Don't forget that the water needs to be boiling before you add the pasta to the saucepan, so begin heating the water a good 10 minutes before you commence cooking.

4. *Al dente* is an Italian phrase used to refer to the desired level of cooking that pasta should have. Translated it means that the pasta should be slightly undercooked and retain a little firmness when bitten.

5. Stir the pasta regularly during cooking because certain pastas float on the surface of the water and will not cook thoroughly unless stirred.

6. When the pasta is cooked, drain it very thoroughly in a colander and give it a gentle shake as cooking water can collect in the more shapely varieties.

7. Return the cooked pasta to its saucepan until you are ready to serve; this will help keep it hot.

Finally, an important point. Your chosen sauce should complement the pasta, not dominate it. Add sufficient sauce, a spoonful at a time, until you feel the balance between pasta and sauce is a good one. Any spare sauce can be refrigerated and used later.

Fettuccine with Chicken & Avocado

SERVES 4

The red pesto and green avocado make this dish very colorful

INGREDIENTS
2 cloves garlic, crushed
juice and rind of 1 lemon
olive oil
salt and freshly ground black pepper
4 skinless chicken breasts
2 slightly under-ripe avocados
1 pound fresh fettuccine
2 tablespoons red pesto

Prepare a simple marinade using the crushed garlic, the juice and rind of the lemon, 3 tablespoons of olive oil and plenty of seasoning.

Make deep cuts into the flesh of the chicken breasts and place them in a bowl, pour over the marinade and toss briefly to ensure they are thoroughly coated. Leave to marinate for at least a couple of hours.

When they are ready, arrange the chicken breasts on a broiler pan and brush with any remaining marinade. Season generously with black pepper.

Cut the avocados in half lengthways. Carefully separate the halves, remove the stones and discard. Remove the skin and slice each half thinly, rub with a little lemon juice to prevent discoloration and set to one side.

Place the marinated chicken breasts under a preheated broiler and cook until they are beginning to brown and the juices run clear. Turn once or twice during cooking.

While the chicken is broiling, bring a large saucepan of lightly salted water to a boil and cook the fettuccine until just tender *(al dente)*. Drain the pasta thoroughly in a colander and toss it with the pesto until it is evenly coated.

Divide the pasta among 4 warmed plates and fan out each avocado half in the center of the pasta.

Place a broiled chicken breast on top of the avocado and then sprinkle with a little of the cooking juices.

Serve immediately with lots of fresh black pepper.

TIME: Preparation takes about 30 minutes, plus marinating.
Cooking takes approximately 15 minutes.

Lamb & Pistachio Nut Sauce

SERVES 4

The red tagliatelle makes this dish very colorful

INGREDIENTS

1 pound fresh lamb fillet, sliced
into 1/2-inch rounds
5 tablespoons apple juice
2 tablespoons clear honey
salt and freshly ground black pepper
2 x 6-inch fresh rosemary stalks
1 pound red tagliatelle
2 tablespoons olive oil
1 bunch scallions, chopped
2 ounces pistachio nuts, chopped

Place the slices of lamb fillet in a mixing bowl and pour over the apple juice and clear honey. Season well, add the rosemary stalks and mix together thoroughly. Cover and leave to refrigerate for at least a couple of hours.

When the lamb has marinated sufficiently, bring a large saucepan of lightly salted water to a boil and cook the tagliatelle for approximately 5 minutes until just tender *(al dente)*. Drain the cooked pasta thoroughly and then return it to the saucepan to keep warm.

Remove the lamb from the marinade and drain well. Heat the olive oil in a skillet and add the lamb one piece at a time, ensuring each browns and seals in the flavor as quickly as possible. Turn the lamb over and brown the other side.

When all the lamb has sealed, add the chopped scallions and pistachios and fry them briefly with the lamb. When the onion begins to soften, add a few tablespoons of the marinade to make a small amount of sauce and adjust the seasoning.

Add the contents of the skillet to the hot pasta and toss together briefly. Transfer to a warmed dish and serve immediately.

TIME: Preparation takes about 20 minutes, plus marinating.
Cooking takes approximately 20 minutes.

14

Spaghetti with Parma Ham & Peas

SERVES 4

Stuffed pasta can be enhanced by serving with this sauce

INGREDIENTS

2 tablespoons olive oil

1 medium onion, finely chopped

4 ounces sliced Parma ham, cut into pieces

6 ounces frozen peas, defrosted

salt and freshly ground black pepper

1 pound fresh spaghetti

1¼ cups heavy cream

3 ounces freshly grated Parmesan cheese

▊ Heat the olive oil in a medium-sized saucepan and cook the chopped onion until it softens and browns lightly.

▊ Add the pieces of Parma ham and stir into the onion for a minute, then add the peas and stir for one more minute. Be gentle at this stage because the peas are quite delicate.

▊ Bring a large saucepan of lightly salted water to a boil and cook the spaghetti for approximately 3 minutes until just tender *(al dente)*. Drain the pasta thoroughly in a colander.

▊ Gently heat the cream in a small saucepan but do not allow it to boil.

▊ Put the drained pasta back into its saucepan and season well. Add the Parma ham mixture and the hot cream and toss them all together until well combined.

▊ Transfer the finished pasta into a presentable heatproof bowl and sprinkle thickly with the grated Parmesan. Place under a preheated broiler for a few minutes until the cheese has melted and browned a little, then take it immediately to the table.

TIME: Preparation takes about 15 minutes. Cooking takes approximately 25 minutes.

Bacon & Walnut

SERVES *4*

This is the crunchiest of sauces!

INGREDIENTS
2 tablespoons olive oil
8 slices smoked bacon, rind removed
salt and freshly ground black pepper
1 pound fresh spaghetti
4 tablespoons walnut oil
4 ounces shelled walnuts, roughly chopped
2 tablespoons snipped chives

▌Heat the olive oil in a skillet and fry the bacon slices, turning regularly, until they are brown and very crispy.
▌While the bacon is cooking, bring a large saucepan of lightly salted water to a boil and cook the fresh spaghetti for approximately 3 minutes until the pasta is just tender *(al dente)*.
▌Drain the pasta thoroughly in a colander and return it to the saucepan, add the walnut oil and some black pepper and toss until the spaghetti is well coated.
▌Break up the fried bacon and add to the pan along with the chopped walnuts and snipped chives. Toss again very briefly and serve immediately on a warmed dish.

TIME: *Preparation takes about 5 minutes.*
Cooking takes approximately 10 minutes.

Basil & Prosciutto

SERVES *4*

Without doubt, pasta and fresh basil were made for each other

INGREDIENTS
1 pound fresh penne
2 tablespoons olive oil
1 clove garlic, chopped
8 ounces Prosciutto (or any lean ham), chopped
1 ounce fresh basil leaves
4 tablespoons thick Greek yogurt
salt and freshly ground black pepper

▌Bring a large saucepan of lightly salted water to a boil and cook the fresh penne for approximately 5 minutes until just tender *(al dente)*.
▌While the pasta is cooking, heat the olive oil in a skillet and briefly fry the garlic until it begins to brown. Add the chopped prosciutto and fry for two or three minutes until it too just begins to brown. Remove the pan from the heat.
▌Drain the cooked pasta in a colander and tip it back into the saucepan. Roughly tear the basil leaves and add to the pan along with the fried prosciutto and garlic.
▌Season generously and toss the pasta to mix the ingredients. Spoon the yogurt into the hot pasta and stir until lightly coated. Transfer to a warmed dish and serve.

TIME: *Preparation takes about 10 minutes.*
Cooking takes approximately 10 minutes.

16

Tagliatelle with Chicken and Samphire

SERVES 4

As samphire has only a short season you could use asparagus as a substitute

INGREDIENTS
1 pound freshly picked samphire
salt and freshly ground black pepper
4 pints fresh chicken stock
1 pound fresh tagliatelle
butter

▌Wash the samphire under cold running water and remove any rough-looking pieces. Bring a saucepan of lightly salted water to a boil and cook the samphire for approximately 3 minutes until the flesh is just tender.

▌While the samphire is cooking, bring the chicken stock to a boil and add the tagliatelle. Leave to cook for 5 minutes, stirring regularly, until the pasta is just tender *(al dente)*.

▌Drain the pasta thoroughly and return it to the saucepan, add a good knob of butter and plenty of black pepper and toss together briefly to melt the butter.

▌Drain the samphire thoroughly and add a little butter and black pepper.

▌Serve the pasta on 4 warmed plates and share the samphire evenly among them. The correct way to eat samphire is to pick it up with your fingers and suck the flesh from the central core, which can then be discarded. Serving this unusual vegetable with pasta is a real luxury and a great excuse to lick your fingers afterwards!

TIME: Preparation takes about 5 minutes. Cooking takes approximately 15 minutes.

COOK'S TIP: Samphire is indigenous to Europe and has a short season running from August to early October. Of the two varieties, rock and marsh, marsh samphire is the most tender and, as the name suggests, grows in waterlogged ground.

18

Flash-fried Marinated Steak Sauce

SERVES 4

Good-quality meat needs frying for only the briefest of time

INGREDIENTS

1 tablespoon Dijon mustard

²/₃ cup natural yogurt

1 tablespoon ground cumin

2 tablespoons chopped cilantro

salt and freshly ground black pepper

1 pound fresh sirloin steak, cut into thin slices

1 pound fresh tagliatelle

2 tablespoons olive oil

5 tablespoons white wine

fresh cilantro to garnish

▌Prepare the marinade by mixing together the Dijon mustard, yogurt, ground cumin, chopped cilantro and seasoning. Stir the marinade into the sliced steak, cover and leave to stand for at least an hour for the flavors to infuse.

▌When the steak has marinated sufficiently, bring a large saucepan of lightly salted water to a boil and begin cooking the tagliatelle until just tender (*al dente*).

▌While the pasta is cooking, heat the olive oil in a skillet and fry a few strips of steak at a time on each side until they begin to brown. Remove the cooked steak from the skillet and keep warm while the rest is being fried. Once all the steak is cooked, lower the heat under the skillet.

▌Drain the cooked pasta in a colander, return it to the saucepan and toss it with the fried steak. Transfer it to a warmed serving dish.

▌Increase the heat under the skillet for a few seconds and splash in the white wine – this will loosen any cooking juices adhering to the pan and add to the flavor of the finished dish.

▌Allow the wine to reduce by half, then pour it over the pasta. Garnish with some roughly chopped fresh cilantro and serve immediately.

TIME: Preparation takes about 10 minutes, plus marinating.
Cooking takes approximately 25 minutes.

19

Beef & Red Peppers

SERVES 4

*Using black pasta adds an air of mystery
to this dish*

INGREDIENTS
salt and freshly ground black pepper
1 pound black fettuccine
2 tablespoons olive oil
2 cloves garlic, thinly sliced
2 red bell peppers, seeded and diced
1 pound good-quality steak, thinly sliced
4 tablespoons oyster sauce

Bring a large saucepan of lightly salted water to a boil and cook the fettuccine for approximately 5 minutes until just tender *(al dente)*. Drain the pasta thoroughly and keep warm in the saucepan.

Heat the olive oil in a saucepan or wok and fry the garlic for a minute until it just begins to brown. Add the chopped red bell pepper and then fry for a further minute until it begins to soften slightly.

Add the sliced steak and cook until sealed and lightly browned. Add the oyster sauce and lots of pepper and stir it into the meat until the steak is well coated.

Add the steak and sauce to the black fettuccine and toss them together until well combined. Transfer to a warmed dish and serve immediately.

TIME: Preparation takes about 10 minutes.
Cooking takes approximately 10 minutes.

Bacon & Eggs

SERVES 4–6

This can be prepared well in advance

INGREDIENTS
1 pound dried pasta shells (conchiglie)
salt and freshly ground black pepper
olive oil
8 ounces rindless bacon, unsmoked
2 ounces shelled pistachios, roughly chopped
4 chopped hard boiled eggs
4 tablespoons Greek yogurt

Cook the pasta shells in plenty of boiling salted water, stirring occasionally, until just tender *(al dente)*. Drain off the cooking water and toss the pasta in a little olive oil. Allow to cool completely.

Arrange bacon on a wire rack placed in a pan so that all the cooking juices are collected below. Place under a preheated boiler and cook, turning regularly, until very crisp. Allow to cool on some paper towel.

Place the cooked pasta in a large, presentable bowl, add the chopped eggs and pistachios and season well.

Gently toss to lightly mix the ingredients and add sufficient Greek yogurt, a tablespoon at a time, to bind together. Just before serving, crumble the bacon and sprinkle it over the top.

TIME: Preparation takes about 10 minutes.
Cooking takes approximately 10 minutes.

21

Spicy Meatballs on Herbed Spaghetti

SERVES 4

This famous dish should not be overlooked, it is as tasty as ever

INGREDIENTS

1 pound fresh spaghetti
1 tablespoon chopped fresh parsley
1 tablespoon chopped fresh basil

FOR THE MEATBALLS

1 pound fresh lean ground beef
2 cups white breadcrumbs
1 teaspoon dried oregano
2 eggs, lightly beaten
salt and freshly ground black pepper
4 tablespoons olive oil for frying

FOR THE SAUCE

14-ounce can chopped tomatoes
1 tablespoon clear honey
2 tablespoons olive oil

❚ Place the ground beef, breadcrumbs, oregano, beaten eggs and seasoning in a mixing bowl. Using your hands, mix together until well combined. If the mixture is too sloppy add some more breadcrumbs.

❚ Lightly rub a little flour over the palms of the hands and break off walnut-sized pieces of mixture. Roll them between the hands until they are ball shaped; this quantity should yield approximately 20 meatballs. Set aside while you prepare the sauce.

❚ Pour the can of tomatoes through a sieve to remove all the seeds and any remaining skin. Place in a saucepan and stir in the honey and olive oil, then place over a medium heat and allow to simmer for 10–15 minutes to reduce and thicken.

❚ Heat 2 tablespoons of olive oil and begin frying the meatballs a few at a time until they are golden brown all over. Carefully remove the cooked meatballs from the skillet and keep them warm in the oven.

❚ Having fried half the meatballs, pour the oil from the skillet and give it a quick wipe out with a few sheets of paper towel. Pour in the rest of the olive oil and continue frying the remaining meatballs.

❚ Bring a large saucepan of salted water to a boil and cook the spaghetti for approximately 5 minutes or until just tender (*al dente*).

❚ Thoroughly drain the pasta and toss it with the chopped fresh herbs. Arrange on a large oval serving plate and place the meatballs in the center. Spoon over lots of hot tomato sauce and serve immediately.

TIME: Preparation takes about 25 minutes. Cooking takes approximately 35 minutes.

22

Sausage & Tomato Sauce

SERVES 4

This is an excellent dish for a quick supper

INGREDIENTS
4 tablespoons olive oil
1 medium onion, finely chopped
2 cloves garlic, chopped
6 ounces Italian sausage, roughly chopped
14-ounce can chopped tomatoes
1 tablespoon tomato paste
1 tablespoon clear honey
salt and freshly ground black pepper
1 pound pasta of your choice
freshly grated Parmesan cheese to sprinkle

Heat 2 tablespoons of the olive oil in a saucepan and fry the onion and garlic until softening and just beginning to brown.

Add the chopped sausage and continue frying for a couple of minutes until the sausage has heated right through.

Lower the heat and add the chopped tomatoes, tomato paste and honey. Stir to combine them with the onion and season well. Leave to simmer uncovered for 10–15 minutes so the sauce can reduce and thicken a little.

Bring a pan of salted water to a boil and cook the pasta until just tender *(al dente)*. If the pasta you have chosen is fresh, this will take about 5 minutes. Dried pasta will take roughly twice as long.

When cooked, drain the pasta thoroughly in a colander and toss it in a bowl with the remaining olive oil and plenty of pepper.

Arrange the pasta on 1 large serving plate or 4 individual ones and spoon the sauce over the top. Serve with a large bowl of fresh Parmesan.

TIME: Preparation takes about 15 minutes. Cooking takes approximately 35 minutes.

24

Rabbit in Red Wine Sauce

SERVES 4

This rich sauce is excellent with a robust pasta such as pappardelle

INGREDIENTS

12 ounces rabbit meat, boned
1 tablespoon flour
salt and freshly ground black pepper
olive oil
1 medium onion, chopped
2 cloves garlic, chopped
6 slices bacon, rind removed
$^2/_3$ cup red wine
8 ounces ripe tomatoes, roughly chopped
$1^1/_4$ cups vegetable stock
bunch of fresh cilantro
1 pound fresh pappardelle

Cut the rabbit meat into even walnut-sized pieces and place on a clean, dry surface. Season the flour with a little salt and freshly ground black pepper and sprinkle it over the rabbit meat. Roll the meat until well coated and set to one side.

Heat 3 tablespoons of olive oil in a skillet and fry the chopped garlic and onion until softening and beginning to brown. At this point cut the bacon into $^1/_2$ inch lengths and add to the skillet. Continue frying until the bacon turns crispy and golden brown.

Add the floured rabbit meat to the skillet and gently cook until the meat is sealed on all sides and just beginning to turn a lovely golden color.

Turn the heat up briefly and add the red wine; this will deglaze the pan and add flavor to the sauce. Add the chopped tomatoes, stir briefly, then pour in the vegetable stock.

Season the sauce well and add a good handful of fresh cilantro. Leave the sauce to simmer uncovered for about one hour, stirring occasionally, until the rabbit meat is tender and the sauce has reduced and thickened.

Bring a large saucepan of lightly salted water to a boil and cook the pappardelle for about 5 minutes until just tender (*al dente*).

Drain the pasta thoroughly in a colander and return it to the saucepan. Add 2 tablespoons of olive oil and some pepper and toss together briefly until all the pasta is coated. Transfer the pasta to a large warmed serving dish.

Test a little of the sauce on a teaspoon and correct the seasoning if necessary. Spoon the rabbit into the center of the pasta and garnish with lots of fresh cilantro. Serve immediately.

TIME: Preparation takes about 20 minutes.
Cooking takes approximately 1 hour 20 minutes.

Fettuccine Carbonara

SERVES 4

This classic dish is very easy to prepare

INGREDIENTS
1 tablespoon olive oil
8 ounces rindless smoked bacon cut into
$^1/_2$ inch strips
4 eggs
4 ounces freshly grated Parmesan cheese
salt and freshly ground black pepper
1 pound fresh fettuccine
chopped parsley, to garnish

Heat the olive oil in a skillet and fry the strips of bacon until golden and crisp. Depending on the type of bacon, you may need to pour off the juices that collect to enable it to brown. Remove the bacon from the skillet and set to one side.

Break the eggs into a bowl and lightly beat them together, add the grated Parmesan and plenty of seasoning.

Bring a large saucepan of lightly salted water to a boil and cook the fettuccine for approximately 5 minutes or until just tender *(al dente).*

Quickly drain off all the cooking liquid and return the pasta to the saucepan. Add the egg mixture and fried bacon and stir it into the pasta. The heat from the fettuccine will cook the egg.

Adjust the seasoning and transfer the pasta to a heated serving dish. Garnish with some chopped parsley and serve right away.

TIME: Preparation takes about 10 minutes. Cooking takes approximately 20 minutes.

Orecchiette with Chicken & Nutmeg

SERVES 4

Freshly grated nutmeg is an excellent spice to use on pasta

INGREDIENTS
4 chicken breasts, skinned
olive oil
salt and freshly ground black pepper
4 cloves garlic, crushed
1 pound dried orecchiette (pasta shells)
fresh nutmeg for grating
2 tablespoons green pesto

▌Preheat the broiler.

▌Brush the chicken breasts on both sides with olive oil and season well. Smear the garlic over the chicken breasts then place them on a tinfoil-covered broiler pan.

▌Broil the chicken for about 10–15 minutes until it has browned nicely, turning once during cooking.

▌While the chicken is broiling, bring a large pan of lightly salted water to a boil and cook the orecchiette for about 10 minutes until just tender (*al dente*). Drain the pasta thoroughly in a colander.

▌When the chicken is cooked, transfer it to a plate and allow to cool for a few minutes. When cool enough to handle, chop the garlicky chicken into evenly sized pieces and grate over a little fresh nutmeg. Turn the pieces over and repeat.

▌Return the drained pasta to the saucepan and add the green pesto. Toss briefly to coat the orecchiette evenly.

▌Add the nutmeg chicken and a little seasoning and mix into the pasta. Transfer to a warmed serving dish and serve immediately.

TIME: Preparation takes about 20 minutes. Cooking takes approximately 15 minutes.

29

Creamy Lamb & Olive Sauce

SERVES 4

If you prefer, you can use any type of meat you wish

INGREDIENTS

3 tablespoons olive oil

2 cloves garlic, chopped

1 large onion, finely chopped

12 ounces fresh ground lamb

1 tablespoon tomato paste

1¼ cups vegetable stock

salt and freshly ground black pepper

1 pound fresh spaghetti

4 ounces black olives, pitted and sliced

1 ounce pine nuts

1¼ cups heavy cream

chopped fresh mint to garnish

▌Heat the olive oil in a skillet and then fry the chopped garlic and onion until soft. Do not let them brown.

▌Add the ground lamb and fry, stirring continuously, until all the meat is sealed and it is beginning to brown lightly.

▌Stir in the tomato paste, vegetable stock and plenty of seasoning. Simmer over a gentle heat, uncovered, for about 30 minutes, until the meat is tender and the liquid much reduced in quantity and slightly thicker.

▌Bring a large saucepan of lightly salted water to a boil and cook the spaghetti for approximately 3 minutes until just tender *(al dente)*. Drain the pasta thoroughly in a colander and transfer to a warm serving dish.

▌Stir the sliced olives and pine nuts into the meat sauce, then reduce the heat and add the heavy cream. Gently warm the finished sauce through and spoon into the center of the spaghetti.

▌Garnish with chopped fresh mint and serve immediately.

TIME: Preparation takes about 15 minutes. Cooking takes approximately 1 hour.

30

Chicken & Mushroom Sauce

SERVES 4

The classic combination of chicken and mushrooms goes very well with pasta

INGREDIENTS
3 tablespoons olive oil
2 cloves garlic, finely chopped
6 ounces rindless smoked bacon, chopped
6 ounces flat cap mushrooms, sliced
12 ounces cooked chicken, roughly chopped
14-ounce can chopped tomatoes
salt and freshly ground black pepper
1 pound fresh tagliatelle
2 tablespoons green pesto
1 tablespoon snipped chives
freshly grated Parmesan cheese to sprinkle

▌ Heat the olive oil in a skillet and fry the garlic for one minute. Add the chopped bacon and then continue frying until the bacon is crispy and nicely browned.

▌ Add the mushrooms and fry until they have absorbed much of the oil, then add the chopped chicken and tomatoes. Season well, then leave to simmer for about 10 minutes.

▌ Bring a large saucepan of lightly salted water to a boil and cook the tagliatelle for approximately 5 minutes until just tender *(al dente)*. Drain the cooked pasta thoroughly in a colander and return it to the saucepan.

▌ Add the green pesto and snipped chives to the pan and toss with the pasta until evenly coated. Transfer the tagliatelle to a warmed serving dish.

▌ Spoon the finished sauce into the middle of the pasta and serve immediately with plenty of grated Parmesan.

TIME: Preparation takes about 15 minutes. Cooking takes approximately 30 minutes.

31

Chicken Liver & Cannellini Bean Sauce

This hearty combination is just right for a winter supper

INGREDIENTS

12 ounces fresh chicken livers

2 tablespoons flour

salt and freshly ground black pepper

2 tablespoons olive oil

1 medium onion, thinly sliced

14-ounce can chopped tomatoes

7-ounce can cannellini beans, drained

1 pound pasta of your choice

1 tablespoon chopped fresh tarragon

Tarragon leaves to garnish (optional)

Rinse the chicken livers under cold running water and dry them on paper towel. Look over the livers and carefully cut away any white or discolored areas with a sharp knife.

Cut the cleaned livers into approximately 1-inch pieces and roll in the flour to give them a light coating. Season well and set to one side.

Heat the olive oil in a skillet and gently fry the sliced onion until soft and browned lightly.

Add the chicken livers and fry for a minute or two on each side until they are just beginning to brown. Add the chopped tomatoes and cannellini beans and stir in the chopped tarragon and plenty of seasoning.

While the sauce is gently simmering, bring a large saucepan of lightly salted water to a boil and cook the pasta. If you have chosen fresh pasta this will take 3–5 minutes to cook and is ready when just tender *(al dente)*. If you are using dried pasta this will need roughly twice the cooking time.

Drain the cooked pasta thoroughly in a colander and arrange it on a large serving dish.

Taste a little of the sauce on a teaspoon and correct the seasoning if necessary. Spoon the finished sauce into the center of the pasta and serve immediately garnished with a few tarragon leaves, if you wish.

TIME: Preparation takes about 10 minutes. Cooking takes approximately 20 minutes.

Rich Bolognese Sauce

SERVES 4–6

This sauce is best prepared well in advance, as allowing
the sauce to stand intensifies the flavor

INGREDIENTS

4 tablespoons olive oil

2 cloves garlic, chopped

1 medium onion, chopped

1 carrot, chopped

1 stick celery, chopped

3 slices unsmoked bacon, chopped

12 ounces lean ground beef

14-ounce can chopped tomatoes

2 tablespoons tomato paste

salt and freshly ground black pepper

2 teaspoons sugar

1 pound fresh pappardelle

chopped parsley for garnish

freshly grated Parmesan cheese, to sprinkle

Heat the olive oil in a large saucepan, add the garlic, onion, carrot and celery and fry until the onion softens and the vegetables begin to brown.

Add the chopped bacon and ground beef and continue frying until the meat is sealed and beginning to brown nicely.

Stir in the chopped tomatoes and tomato paste and season well. Cover and allow to simmer for approximately 45 minutes, stirring regularly, until the meat is tender and the sauce has reduced and thickened a little. If the sauce becomes a little dry during cooking, add a few tablespoons of cold water to moisten it.

When the sauce is cooked, stir in the sugar and correct the seasoning. If not needed immediately, cover with a tight-fitting lid and set to one side in a cool place until required. This really does improve the overall flavor of the sauce.

When the time has come to finish preparing the dish, bring a large saucepan of salted water to a boil and cook the pappardelle for approximately 5 minutes until it is just tender *(al dente)*. Drain thoroughly in a colander and arrange the pasta on a large serving dish.

Thoroughly reheat the bolognese sauce, taste a little on a teaspoon to check the seasoning and spoon the sauce over the pappardelle. Garnish with lots of fresh chopped parsley and serve immediately with a large bowl of freshly grated Parmesan.

TIME: Preparation takes about 15 minutes, plus standing.

Cooking takes approximately 1 hour.

34

Tagliatelle with Ham & Cream

SERVES 4

If *Parma ham is unavailable, other types of ham or bacon can be used*

INGREDIENTS
4 ounces Parma ham, thinly sliced
1¼ cups heavy cream
4 ounces freshly grated Parmesan cheese
1 tablespoon fresh snipped chives
salt and freshly ground black pepper
1 pound fresh tagliatelle
olive oil
freshly grated Parmesan cheese to sprinkle

Place the Parma ham in a mixing bowl along with the heavy cream, grated Parmesan, snipped chives and plenty of seasoning.

Bring a large saucepan of lightly salted water to a boil and cook the fresh tagliatelle for about 5 minutes, until just tender *(al dente)*.

Drain the cooked pasta in a colander then immediately return it to the saucepan and add 2 tablespoons of olive oil. Toss to coat the pasta thoroughly.

Add the prepared sauce to the hot pasta and toss once more so that the pasta is evenly coated. Transfer to a warmed serving dish and serve immediately with lots of freshly grated Parmesan.

TIME: Preparation takes about 15 minutes. Cooking takes approximately 10 minutes.

35

Fresh Crab & Eggplant Salad

SERVES 6–8

This makes a lovely "extra" on a summer buffet table

INGREDIENTS

2 medium eggplants, cut into ¼-inch slices

salt

12 ounces dried fusilli

olive oil

½ cup grated carrot

1 teaspoon freshly grated ginger

4 ounces white crab meat, loosely broken up

FOR THE DRESSING

6 tablespoons virgin olive oil

2 tablespoons white wine vinegar

½ teaspoon sugar

½ teaspoon English mustard powder

salt and freshly ground black pepper

▌Sprinkle the eggplant slices with a little salt. Set aside for 20 minutes to extract the bitter juices then rinse them under cold water and dry on paper towel.

▌Bring a large saucepan of lightly salted water to a boil and cook the dried pasta according to the package instructions, usually about 10 minutes.

▌When the fusilli is cooked, drain off the cooking liquid very thoroughly and toss the pasta with a little olive oil to prevent sticking. Set aside to cool.

▌Heat 2 tablespoons of olive oil in a skillet and fry a few eggplant slices at a time. Cook until they begin to brown, then turn over and continue cooking until they become soft and transparent. Remove from the skillet and allow to cool on paper towel. Repeat until all the eggplant is cooked.

▌Place the cooked pasta, grated carrot, ginger and crab meat in a mixing bowl. Roughly cut up the cooked eggplant and add to the bowl. Using your hands gently toss the ingredients together.

▌Put all the dressing ingredients in a screw-top jar and shake well. Pour a little at a time onto the salad and toss it until all the ingredients are well coated and there is a small amount of excess liquid in the bottom of the bowl. Any remaining dressing can be refrigerated for a few days.

▌Spoon the salad onto a serving dish and chill lightly before serving.

TIME: Preparation takes about 25 minutes. Cooking takes approximately 20 minutes.

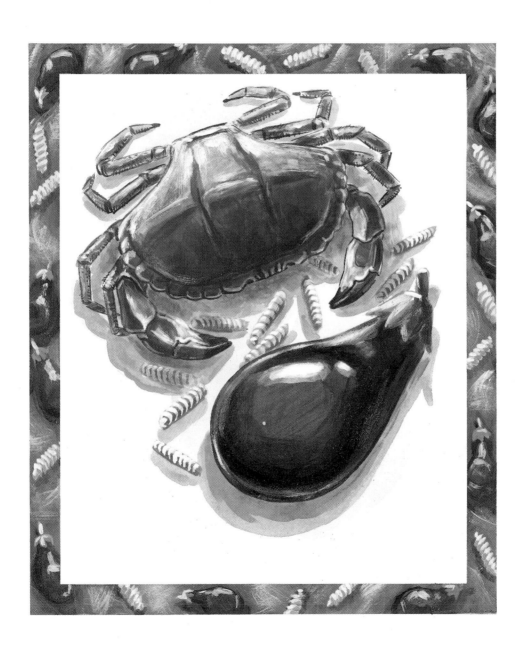

Mixed Seafood Sauce

SERVES 4

Quick to prepare, and looks fantastic

INGREDIENTS
1 tablespoon olive oil
1 medium onion, finely chopped
1-pound package frozen mixed seafood, defrosted
14-ounce can chopped tomatoes
salt and freshly ground black pepper
1 pound fresh red spaghetti (or tagliatelle)
1 tablespoon chopped parsley
freshly grated Parmesan cheese, for sprinkling

▌ Heat the olive oil in a saucepan and lightly fry the chopped onion until soft. Add the package of mixed seafood and stir briefly.
▌ Stir in the chopped tomatoes and season the sauce well. Cover and allow to simmer for approximately 10 minutes.
▌ Bring a large saucepan of lightly salted water to a boil and cook the pasta for 5 minutes until it is just tender *(al dente)*. Drain the cooked pasta thoroughly in a colander and transfer it to a warmed serving dish or divide it among 4 warmed plates.
▌ Spoon the seafood sauce over the pasta and garnish with the chopped parsley. Serve immediately with grated Parmesan.

TIME: Preparation takes about 5 minutes.
Cooking takes approximately 15 minutes.

Fresh Clam Sauce

SERVES 4

Clams have a wonderful flavor

INGREDIENTS
2 tablespoons olive oil
1 medium onion, finely chopped
2 cloves garlic, finely chopped
2 pounds fresh, shelled clams, cleaned
$^2/_3$ cup white wine
salt and freshly ground black pepper
1 pound fresh pappardelle
2 tablespoons chopped fresh parsley, to garnish

▌ Heat the olive oil in a large saucepan and fry the onion and garlic until softened, but not browned.
▌ Add the clams to the saucepan and pour over the white wine, briefly stir together and cover the pan with a tight-fitting lid. Allow approximately 5 minutes for the clams to cook. Discard any shells that do not open.
▌ Bring a large saucepan of lightly salted water to a boil and cook the pappardelle for 5 minutes until just tender *(al dente)*. Drain the cooked pasta thoroughly.
▌ Return the pappardelle to the saucepan and, using a slotted spoon, drain off the clams and add to the pasta. Add the parsley and transfer to a warm serving bowl.
▌ Spoon over some of the cooking liquor from the clams and grind over plenty of pepper to serve.

TIME: Preparation takes about 20 minutes.
Cooking takes approximately 20 minutes.

*M*ussels & *S*un-dried *T*omatoes

*F*resh mussels taste wonderful with pasta

INGREDIENTS

5 pints fresh mussels in shells

²⁄₃ cup white wine

salt

1 pound fresh tagliatelle

4 tablespoons olive oil

2 ounces sun-dried tomatoes, chopped

2 tablespoons chopped parsley

When using fresh mussels it is better to purchase them the day before you want to use them. Wash them thoroughly in cold running water and remove any barnacles that may adhere to the shells. Also remove the clump of fine hair that grows between the shell halves (this is known as the beard).

Put the cleaned mussels in a large bowl and cover them with fresh cold water. Sprinkle a little flour or breadcrumbs on the water's surface; the mussels will feed on this and clean out any grit that may be in the shell. Leave overnight.

The following day drain off the water and rinse the mussels thoroughly in cold water, discard any that have already opened. The mussels are now ready for cooking.

Pour the wine into a large saucepan with a tight-fitting lid, place over a medium heat and when steam starts to rise add the mussels to the pan and cover with the lid. Steam for approximately 5 minutes, stirring occasionally.

While the mussels are steaming, set a large saucepan of salted water to boil and begin cooking the tagliatelle for about 5 minutes or until just tender *(al dente)*.

Remove the saucepan of mussels from the heat and pick out 8 of the best-looking ones to leave in their shells and use as a garnish. Remove the rest from their shells and keep warm.

Heat the olive oil and quickly fry the chopped sun-dried tomatoes until they are heated through.

Drain the cooked tagliatelle thoroughly and add to the saucepan, toss to combine with the tomatoes and to coat the pasta in oil. Stir in the cooked mussels.

Arrange the finished pasta on a large serving dish and garnish with the chopped parsley and reserved shelled mussels. Serve immediately.

TIME: Preparation takes about 10 minutes, plus soaking.

Cooking takes approximately 15 minutes.

Anchovy & Zucchini Sauce

SERVES 4

Fried zucchini has a lovely clean flavor

INGREDIENTS
4 large zucchinis
salt and freshly ground black pepper
1 pound pasta of your choice
4 tablespoons olive oil
2 cloves garlic, peeled and chopped
1 tablespoon freeze-dried thyme
2 cans anchovy fillets in oil

Use a vegetable peeler to remove deep strips of skin from the length of each zucchini at equal distances around the vegetable. Slice the zucchinis into ¼-inch thicknesses. They should have an attractive castellated edge.

Bring a large saucepan of lightly salted water to a boil and cook the pasta until just tender *(al dente)*. If you have chosen dried pasta this will take approximately 10–12 minutes; fresh pasta will take less than half the time.

While the pasta is cooking, heat the olive oil in a skillet and cook the chopped garlic until lightly browned.

Add the sliced zucchinis to the skillet and fry until softened and evenly browned. Just before the zucchini has finish cooking, stir in the dried thyme and plenty of seasoning.

When the pasta is cooked, drain it thoroughly in a colander and return it to the saucepan. Add the anchovies and their oil along with the fried zucchinis and some more seasoning.

Gently toss until well mixed together and transfer to a warmed serving dish. Serve immediately.

TIME: Preparation takes about 10 minutes. Cooking takes approximately 20 minutes.

Haddock & Tomato Sauce

SERVES 4

The *firm texture of the haddock really makes this dish a success*

INGREDIENTS
1 pound fresh haddock
4 tablespoons butter
1 small onion, finely chopped
1 pound ripe plum tomatoes
4 ounces pitted black olives, halved
salt and freshly ground black pepper
1 pound pasta of your choice
sprigs of parsley, to garnish

Place the haddock in a skillet and add sufficient water to just cover the fish. Place the pan over a medium heat and cook the fish until the flesh comes away from the bone easily.

Carefully lift the cooked fish from the liquor and separate the flesh from the bones and skin. Set to one side.

Melt the butter in a saucepan and fry the onion until soft and just beginning to brown. Chop the tomatoes into evenly sized pieces and add to the pan. Season well and cook gently until the tomatoes soften.

Carefully stir in the flaked haddock and chopped olives and keep the sauce warm over a low heat.

Bring a large saucepan of lightly salted water to a boil and cook the pasta. If you are using fresh pasta this will take approximately 5 minutes until just tender (*al dente*). Dried pasta will take roughly twice as long.

Drain the cooked pasta thoroughly and return it to the saucepan, add the haddock and tomato sauce and gently toss them together until they are well mixed.

Transfer the pasta to a warmed serving dish and garnish with a few sprigs of fresh parsley. Serve immediately.

TIME: Preparation takes about 15 minutes. Cooking takes approximately 30 minutes.

43

Roast Pepper & Shrimp Sauce

SERVES 4

This dish is colorful and mouthwateringly delicious

INGREDIENTS
16 large shelled shrimp
1 red, 1 green, 1 yellow bell pepper
olive oil
salt
1 pound fresh pappardelle

FOR THE MARINADE
3 tablespoons olive oil
1 tablespoon light soy sauce
1 clove garlic, crushed
salt and freshly ground black pepper
2 teaspoons tomato paste

▌ Place the marinade ingredients in a screw-top jar and shake thoroughly to combine all the flavors. Lay the shrimp in a shallow bowl and pour over the marinade ensuring that all are covered. Set to one side for at least 30 minutes.

▌ Brush the peppers with a little olive oil and place on a baking sheet in a preheated oven at 350° until the peppers soften and begin to scorch a little. This will take approximately 30–40 minutes.

▌ When the peppers are nearly cooked, place a large saucepan of lightly salted water over a high heat and bring it to a boil. Drop in the fresh pappardelle and cook it for about 5 minutes until just tender *(al dente)*.

▌ While the pasta is cooking, remove the shrimp from their marinade and arrange them on a broiler pan. Place under a preheated broiler and cook for a couple of minutes on each side, brushing with a little marinade when you turn them over.

▌ Remove the peppers from the oven and carefully chop the flesh into uniform sizes, taking care to remove all the seeds while doing so. Add the chopped pepper to the drained pasta and toss together with 2 tablespoons of olive oil and seasoning.

▌ Arrange the pasta on 1 large or 4 individual warmed serving dishes and place the broiled shrimp in the center. Serve immediately.

TIME: Preparation takes about 10 minutes, plus marinating.
Cooking takes approximately 40 minutes.

44

Spaghetti & Anchovy Salad

SERVES 4

This dish is so refreshing on a sultry summer's day

INGREDIENTS
salt and freshly ground black pepper
8 ounces fresh spaghetti
4 tablespoons olive oil
3 ripe beef tomatoes
6 ounces fresh mozzarella cheese
2 cans anchovy fillets in oil
12 basil leaves
2 tablespoons white wine vinegar

Bring a large saucepan of lightly salted water to a boil and cook the spaghetti for approximately 3 minutes until just tender *(al dente)*.

Drain the pasta thoroughly in a colander and sprinkle with a little oil to prevent sticking, season well and set aside to cool completely. When the pasta has cooled, transfer it to a large serving dish.

Slice the tomatoes and mozzarella cheese and arrange them alternately on top of the spaghetti. Pour the oil from the cans of anchovy fillets over the salad and arrange the fillets on top along with the basil leaves, roughly torn to release their wonderful aroma.

Make a very simple dressing by pouring the olive oil and wine vinegar into a screw-top jar. Season with salt and lots of black pepper and shake vigorously to mix together.

Pour the dressing over the finished salad and serve with crusty bread and chilled white wine.

TIME: Preparation takes about 20 minutes. Cooking takes approximately 5 minutes.

Creamy Tuna Sauce

SERVES 4

Tuna is great with pasta

INGREDIENTS

2 tablespoons olive oil

1 medium onion, finely chopped

7-ounce can tuna fish, drained

salt and freshly ground black pepper

1 pound fresh pappardelle

1 1/4 cups light cream

1 tablespoon green pesto

basil leaves to garnish

Heat the olive oil in a saucepan and fry the onion until soft, but not colored.

Using a fork, break up the tuna and add to the onion. Stir briefly until the fish is warmed through.

Bring a large saucepan of lightly salted water to a boil and cook the pasta for about 5 minutes until just tender *(al dente)*.

While the pasta is cooking, lower the heat under the tuna sauce and add the cream and green pesto. Stir them into the fish and heat gently. Do not let the sauce boil.

Drain the cooked pasta thoroughly and return it to the saucepan. Season well and pour in the sauce.

Toss the pasta and sauce together then transfer to a serving dish. Scatter over a few basil leaves and serve immediately.

TIME: *Preparation takes about 10 minutes.*

Cooking takes approximately 20 minutes.

Shrimp & Rocket

SERVES 4

Rocket complements seafood well

INGREDIENTS

2 tablespoons olive oil

1 medium onion, chopped

8 ounces cooked shelled shrimp

2 ounces frozen garden peas, defrosted

2/3 cup heavy cream

salt and freshly ground black pepper

6 ounces fresh rocket

1 pound fresh spaghetti

Heat the olive oil in a saucepan and fry the onion until soft, but not colored.

Lower the heat and add the shrimp and garden peas. Stir gently, then add the cream and seasoning and continue cooking until well heated through.

Place the rocket in a bowl and pour over sufficient boiling water to cover it. Leave for 15 seconds then drain the blanched rocket thoroughly, chop it roughly and set to one side.

Bring a large saucepan of salted water to a boil and cook the spaghetti for about 5 minutes until just tender.

Drain the pasta and toss with the chopped rocket. Arrange on a large serving dish and spoon over the shrimp sauce. Serve immediately.

TIME: *Preparation takes about 10 minutes.*

Cooking takes approximately 15 minutes.

47

Citrus Butter & Smoked Salmon

SERVES 4

Flavored butters are great fun to use in cooking but are best
prepared several hours before use

INGREDIENTS

1 cup unsalted butter, softened
zest and juice of 2 large limes
salt and freshly ground black pepper
olive oil
1 pound fresh penne
8 ounces fresh smoked salmon, thinly sliced
fresh chives, to garnish

Remove the butter from the refrigerator about an hour before you want to make the citrus butter; this will make it much easier to handle.

Place the softened butter in a bowl and add the juice and zest of the limes and a few good twists of black pepper. Beat together until well combined.

Tear off a sheet of greaseproof paper approximately 12 inches in length and pile the citrus butter in a line across one end, about 2 inches from the edge.

Fold the end of the paper over the butter and roll it tightly into a sausage shape. Carefully twist the ends of the paper in opposite directions to tighten the roll; this will force the butter into a neat log. Refrigerate immediately for a few hours until firm.

Bring a large saucepan of salted water to a boil, add a few drops of oil to prevent the pasta from sticking together and add the fresh penne. Cook until the pasta is still slightly firm then drain in a colander.

Tip the drained pasta into a mixing bowl and add a few $1/2$ inch slices of the citrus butter log. Grind in a little pepper and toss the penne until the butter has melted and coated the pasta.

Mix in the smoked salmon and divide the finished pasta among 4 warmed dishes. Garnish with a few freshly snipped chives and serve immediately.

The remaining citrus log can be returned to the refrigerator for future use.

TIME: *Preparation of citrus log takes about 20 minutes, plus standing and refrigeration. Cooking takes approximately 10 minutes.*

48

Salmon & Toasted Almonds

SERVES 4

Pasta and salmon could have been made for each other

INGREDIENTS

4 x 4-ounce fresh salmon steaks
olive oil
sea salt and freshly ground black pepper
2 tablespoons slivered almonds
1 pound fresh spaghetti
2 tablespoons fresh cilantro, chopped

Cover a broiler pan with tinfoil and arrange the salmon steaks on it. Brush the fish lightly with a little olive oil and season with sea salt and pepper.

Place under a preheated broiler and cook until the fish are just beginning to brown. Carefully turn the steaks over, brush with a little more oil and continue broiling until the salmon flesh can be easily flaked. The whole cooking process should take no more than 10–15 minutes.

Spread the almonds over a baking sheet and when the salmon has finished cooking, quickly place the almonds under the broiler to toast lightly. It is a good idea to stay with the almonds until ready since they burn easily and may need moving around to prevent scorching.

Bring a large saucepan of lightly salted water to a boil and cook the spaghetti for about 3 minutes until just tender *(al dente)*.

While the pasta is cooking, carefully remove the skin from the salmon and break the flesh into natural flakes.

Drain the cooked pasta thoroughly in a colander and return it to the saucepan. Add the chopped cilantro, plenty of seasoning, a little olive oil and roughly half the flaked salmon and gently toss together until well combined.

Transfer the pasta to a large, warmed serving dish and pile the remaining warm salmon flakes in the center of the pasta.

Sprinkle generously with the toasted slivered almonds and serve immediately.

TIME: Preparation takes about 15 minutes. Cooking takes approximately 25 minutes.

Spaghetti with Steamed Mussels

SERVES 4

Fresh mussels are best served with a very simple sauce

INGREDIENTS

2 tablespoons olive oil
1 medium onion, finely chopped
14-ounce can chopped tomatoes
1 tablespoon clear honey
salt and freshly ground black pepper
3 pounds fresh mussels, cleaned
1 pound fresh spaghetti
freshly chopped parsley, to garnish

Heat the olive oil in a saucepan and fry the onion until softened. Add the chopped tomatoes, honey and some salt and black pepper and allow the sauce to simmer for 10 minutes to reduce and thicken slightly. Keep the sauce warm.

Put sufficient cold water to cover the base into a saucepan with a tight-fitting lid and place over the heat. Once it starts producing steam add the cleaned mussels and cover. Allow them to cook for approximately 5 minutes until the mussel shells have opened.

Remove the saucepan from the heat and leave the mussels to cool for a few minutes so you can handle them. Remove them from their shells and drop into the tomato sauce. Discard any shells that have not opened.

Bring a large saucepan of lightly salted water to a boil and cook the spaghetti for approximately 3 minutes until just tender *(al dente)*.

Return the pasta to its saucepan and add the tomato and mussel sauce. Toss them together until well combined then transfer them to a warmed serving dish.

Garnish with chopped parsley and serve immediately.

TIME: Preparation takes about 10 minutes. Cooking takes approximately 25 minutes.

51

Spaghetti with Squid & Asparagus

SERVES 4

Fresh squid has a wonderful taste and texture

INGREDIENTS

12 ounces fresh squid, cleaned and prepared
sifted and seasoned flour for coating
2 egg yolks, loosely beaten
fine breadcrumbs for coating
oil for deep frying
salt and freshly ground black pepper
1 pound fresh spaghetti
6 ounces fresh asparagus
4 tablespoons butter
juice of 1 lemon

Buy clean and prepare the fresh squid. For this dish the bodies should be sliced across into $1/2$-inch-wide rings and the tentacles chopped into similar-sized pieces.

Place 3 shallow bowls in a row. Put the flour in the first, the egg yolks in the second and breadcrumbs in the third. Pass the prepared squid through the bowls until they are all lightly coated in breadcrumbs.

Pour the oil into a pan suitable for deep frying and begin heating until there is just a slight trace of smoke rising from the surface. Begin frying the breadcrumbed squid rings 6 at a time until they are golden brown and crispy. Keep them warm in a low oven.

Bring a large and a small saucepan of lightly salted water to a boil, and drop the fresh spaghetti into the large one and the asparagus into the small. The spaghetti will take approximately 3 minutes to cook and should be just tender *(al dente)*. The asparagus will take about 6 minutes and should remain a little crunchy.

Thoroughly drain the pasta in a colander and transfer it to a serving dish. Cut the asparagus into 1-inch lengths and toss with the spaghetti, butter and lots of black pepper.

Scatter the deep-fried squid over the spaghetti and sprinkle with the lemon juice. Serve immediately.

TIME: *Preparation takes about 20 minutes. Cooking takes approximately 15 minutes.*

53

Broccoli & Fava Bean Sauce

SERVES 4

*A*ny leftover cheese may be used for this sauce

INGREDIENTS
4 tablespoons butter
2 tablespoons flour
1¼ cups fresh milk
4 ounces Red Leicester cheese, grated
salt and freshly ground black pepper
a little grated nutmeg
8 ounces broccoli flowerets
1 pound fresh penne
6 ounces cooked fava beans
freshly grated Parmesan cheese, to sprinkle

❚ Place half the butter in a saucepan and melt gently over a low heat. Add the flour and stir continuously for a few minutes to allow the flour to cook, but not color.

❚ Add the milk a little at a time to begin with, stirring to combine it with the mixture, then increase the flow until all the milk is incorporated and the sauce is smooth.

❚ Add the grated cheese and season well. Add a little grated nutmeg. Whisk over a low heat until all the cheese has melted and the sauce has become pale orange.

❚ Whisk in the remaining butter to give the sauce a glossy appearance and set to one side.

❚ Bring a saucepan of salted water to a boil and blanch the broccoli flowerets for approximately 5 minutes until just tender. Carefully transfer the flowerets to a colander and drain thoroughly.

❚ Bring a large saucepan of lightly salted water to a boil and cook the fresh penne for about 5 minutes, until just tender *(al dente)*. Drain the cooked pasta thoroughly.

❚ Toss the broccoli flowerets and fava beans with the pasta and season well. Quickly reheat the cheese sauce until very hot and carefully fold it into the pasta and vegetables.

❚ Transfer the finished pasta to a warmed serving dish and serve immediately with lots of freshly grated Parmesan.

TIME: Preparation takes about 10 minutes.
Cooking takes approximately 30 minutes.

Cornish Cream & Watercress Sauce

S E R V E S 4

This is a delicious sauce for those who don't need to count calories!

I N G R E D I E N T S
salt and freshly ground black pepper
olive oil
1 pound dried linguine
2 bunches watercress
1¼ cups fresh Cornish cream
2 ounces pine nuts
freshly grated Parmesan cheese, to sprinkle

Bring a large saucepan of lightly salted water to a boil, add a few drops of oil and cook the pasta for approximately 10 minutes until just tender *(al dente)*.

While the pasta is cooking, pick over the watercress to remove any rough-looking leaves and put the remainder in a bowl. Pour over sufficient freshly boiling water to cover and leave to stand for about 30 seconds. Drain off the water and set the blanched watercress to one side.

When the pasta is ready, thoroughly drain off the cooking water and tip the cooked linguine back into the saucepan.

Season well and add the Cornish cream. Place the saucepan over a very low heat and gently toss the cream and pasta together until well combined.

Add the pine nuts and blanched watercress and briefly stir into the sauce until heated through.

Add a little more seasoning if required and serve immediately with generous quantities of grated Parmesan.

TIME: Preparation takes about 5 minutes. Cooking takes approximately 15 minutes.

Sugar Snap Sauce

SERVES 4

These delicious crunchy peas are full of sweet flavor

INGREDIENTS
8 ounces sugar snap peas, trimmed
1 pound fresh pappardelle
²/₃ cup heavy cream
4 ounces freshly grated Parmesan cheese
salt and freshly ground pepper

▌ Place the sugar snaps in a saucepan with a tight-fitting lid. Add just enough water to cover the bottom and set over a medium heat until just cooked but still crunchy. Drain and keep warm.
▌ Bring a saucepan of salted water to a boil and cook the pappardelle until just tender *(al dente);* this will take approximately 5 minutes.
▌ Pour the cream into a saucepan and heat gently; do not let it boil.
▌ Drain off the cooking liquid from the pasta and place it in a large serving bowl along with the cooked sugar snaps, warmed cream, grated cheese and plenty of seasoning.
▌ Toss together until well combined and serve.

TIME: Preparation takes about 10 minutes. Cooking takes approximately 15 minutes.

Chili Oil Sauce

SERVES 4

The very best virgin olive oil is essential for this quick and easy dish

INGREDIENTS
1 pound fresh spaghetti
²/₃ cup extra virgin olive oil
3 red chilies, seeded and finely chopped
pinch of chili powder
freshly ground black pepper

▌ Bring a large saucepan of salted water to a boil and cook the spaghetti for about 5 minutes until just tender *(al dente)*. Thoroughly drain off the cooking liquid in a colander.
▌ Heat 2 tablespoons of the olive oil in a small saucepan and fry the chopped chili briefly to allow the flavor to begin infusing. Add the remaining oil and chili powder and continue heating until the oil has thoroughly warmed through; do not let it boil.
▌ Put the drained spaghetti in a large serving bowl and pour in the warmed olive oil, grind in lots of black pepper and toss together until well combined. Serve immediately.

TIME: Preparation takes about 5 minutes, Cooking takes approximately 10 minutes.

Farfalle with Celery & Apricot Sauce

SERVES 4–6

This attractive dish makes an excellent dinner party starter

INGREDIENTS
4 ounces dried apricots
salt and freshly ground black pepper
12 ounces dried farfalle (pasta bows)
2 tablespoons olive oil
3 sticks celery, washed and chopped
3 ounces freshly grated Parmesan cheese
12 fresh basil leaves

Place the apricots in a bowl and pour over sufficient boiling water to just cover them. Set aside and leave to soak for at least an hour.

Bring a large saucepan of lightly salted water to a boil and cook the dried pasta for approximately 10 minutes until just tender *(al dente)*.

While the pasta is cooking, prepare the simple sauce. Heat the olive oil in a skillet and fry the celery until it begins to soften.

Drain the apricots and chop to a similar size as the celery, add to the skillet and stir together for a couple of minutes. Season well and remove the skillet from the heat.

Drain the cooked pasta thoroughly in a colander and return it to the saucepan, add the grated Parmesan and toss with the hot pasta until it begins to melt and coat the individual pieces.

Add the celery and apricot sauce to the pan along with the basil leaves, mix them into the pasta until well distributed. Finish with a good twist of black pepper and serve immediately.

TIME: Preparation takes about 30 minutes, plus soaking.
Cooking takes approximately 20 minutes.

59

Four Cheese Sauce with Caramelized Onions

SERVES 4–6

This rich sauce is perfect for a special occasion or celebration

60

INGREDIENTS

2 tablespoons butter

2 tablespoons flour

1/2 teaspoon English mustard powder

1 1/4 cups fresh milk

1 ounce grated Parmesan cheese

1 ounce grated mozzarella cheese

1 ounce chopped Gorgonzola cheese

1 ounce Ricotta Cheese

salt and freshly ground black pepper

grated nutmeg

1 pound fresh penne

4 tablespoons unsalted butter

2 large onions, thinly sliced

1 tablespoon superfine sugar

Melt the butter in a saucepan over a low heat. Add the flour and mustard powder and stir continuously for a minute or two.

Add the milk a little at a time, stirring to ensure the sauce is smooth, then increase the flow until all the milk is used and the sauce has a good coating consistency.

Add the four cheeses, and season well. Whisk the sauce until all the cheese has melted and the sauce is beautifully smooth. Add a little grated nutmeg and set the sauce to one side.

Bring a large saucepan of lightly salted water to a boil and cook the fresh penne for about 5 minutes until just tender *(al dente)*.

Melt the unsalted butter in a skillet and fry the onions until soft and just beginning to brown, then sprinkle over the sugar and continue frying the onions until evenly glazed with caramel. Set to one side.

Drain the cooked penne thoroughly and return it to the saucepan. Briefly reheat the cheese sauce to ensure it is piping hot and pour it over the pasta.

Toss the pasta and sauce together until well combined then transfer to a warmed serving dish. Spoon the caramelized onions into the center of the pasta and serve immediately.

TIME: Preparation takes about 15 minutes. Cooking takes approximately 35 minutes.

Pastis & Spinach Tagliatelle

SERVES 4

Spinach and aniseed is a superb combination of flavors

INGREDIENTS
salt and freshly ground black pepper
1 pound fresh spinach tagliatelle
2 pounds fresh young spinach
1 tablespoon olive oil
1 fennel bulb, finely chopped
2 ounces pine nuts
I measure Pernod
1 tablespoon chopped dill to garnish

▌ Bring a saucepan of lightly salted water to a boil and cook the tagliatelle until just tender *(al dente)*.
▌ While the pasta is cooking pick over the spinach, break off any thick stems and remove any rough-looking leaves.
▌ Drain the cooked pasta thoroughly in a colander and return it to the saucepan to keep warm.

▌ To make the sauce, heat the olive oil in a wok or large saucepan. Add the chopped fennel and fry for about 1 minute then add the pine nuts and briefly toss them in the oil.
▌ Add the cleaned spinach and quickly turn it in the wok or saucepan for a few seconds until it wilts. Immediately remove the pan from the heat and sprinkle over the measure of Pernod. Toss to combine it with the other ingredients.
▌ Spoon the sauce into the pan with the cooked tagliatelle, grind over lots of pepper and lightly toss together until well mixed.
▌ Transfer the finished pasta to a warmed serving dish, garnish generously with chopped dill and serve immediately.

TIME: Preparation takes about 15 minutes. Cooking takes approximately 10 minutes.

61

Tagliatelle with Red Cabbage & Chili

SERVES 4

Crunchy sweet red cabbage tastes superb with pasta and chili

INGREDIENTS
1 medium red onion, thinly sliced
12 ounces fresh red cabbage, thinly sliced
3 red chilies, seeded and chopped
2 ounces raisins
1 tablespoon soft brown sugar
freshly ground black pepper
olive oil
1 pound fresh tagliatelle
4 tablespoons heavy cream

Place the onion, cabbage and chili in a saucepan and add sufficient cold water to just cover the base of the pan. Cover and place over a medium heat, stirring occasionally, until both the cabbage and onion soften.

Remove the saucepan from the heat and stir in the raisins and sprinkle over the brown sugar. Replace the lid and set to one side.

Bring a large saucepan of salted water to a boil, add a few drops of oil to prevent sticking and cook the pasta for about 5 minutes until just tender *(al dente)*.

Pour the cooked pasta into a colander to drain off the cooking liquid, then tip it back into the saucepan and add the cream, tossing to coat thoroughly.

Divide the tagliatelle among 4 warmed plates or bowls and using a slotted spoon to drain off any cooking juices, place a generous quantity of red cabbage into the center of each portion. Twist some fresh black pepper over each and serve right away.

TIME: *Preparation takes about 10 minutes. Cooking takes approximately 20 minutes.*

62

Sharp Berry Sauce

SERVES 4

This unusual combination of flavors goes particularly well with cold meats

INGREDIENTS

4 ounces fresh or frozen blueberries
2 ounces fresh or frozen redcurrants
salt and freshly ground black pepper
1 pound fresh tagliatelle

▌ If using fresh fruit, wash thoroughly and remove any stems. Place the fruit in a saucepan with just sufficient cold water to cover the base, cover the saucepan and place over a low heat. Cook until the fruit starts to break up and the juices begin to run. Remove the saucepan from the heat and set to one side.

▌ Bring a large saucepan of lightly salted water to a boil and cook the tagliatelle for approximately 5 minutes until just tender *(al dente)*.

▌ Drain the pasta thoroughly, return it to the saucepan and season it with plenty of black pepper. Add the softened fruit and toss with the pasta until well combined.

▌ Transfer to a warmed dish and serve.

TIME: Preparation takes about 5 minutes.
Cooking time takes approximately 15 minutes.

Fennel & Horseradish Salad

SERVES 4

A refreshing summer salad

INGREDIENTS

salt and freshly ground black pepper
1 pound dried pasta shells (conchiglie)
olive oil
1 large fennel bulb, finely chopped
3 ounces unsalted peanuts
2 tablespoons fresh cilantro, chopped
1 tablespoon cream of horseradish sauce
4 tablespoons Greek yogurt

▌ Bring a large saucepan of lightly salted water to a boil and cook the conchiglie for approximately 10 minutes until just tender *(al dente)*.

▌ Drain well and shake to remove any water that has collected in the shells. Toss in a little olive oil and set aside to cool.

▌ When the pasta has cooled, transfer to a serving bowl and add the fennel, peanuts and cilantro. Toss together well.

▌ Beat the cream of horseradish and lots of black pepper into the Greek yogurt. Add the mixture, a tablespoon at a time, to the pasta to bind it together well.

TIME: Preparation takes about 10 minutes.
Cooking takes approximately 15 minutes.

65

Blue Cheese & Pine Nuts

SERVES 4

Melted blue cheese imparts a lovely strong flavor to this dish

INGREDIENTS
salt and freshly ground black pepper
12 ounces dried conchiglie
2 tablespoons olive oil
1 clove garlic, crushed
4 ounces button mushrooms, thinly sliced
4 ounces blue Stilton cheese, cut into small cubes
2 tablespoons butter
4 tablespoons heavy cream
3 ounces pine nuts

Bring a large saucepan of salted water to a boil and cook the pasta shells for approximately 10 minutes, stirring occasionally, until just tender *(al dente)*.

While the pasta is cooking, heat the olive oil in a skillet and briefly fry the crushed garlic. Add the sliced mushrooms and continue frying until they have softened.

Put the Stilton, butter and cream in a saucepan and place it over a low heat. Stir continually until the cheese has melted and it forms a smooth sauce. Do not let the sauce boil.

Strain the cooked pasta in a colander and shake it well.

Return the conchiglie to the saucepan and add the sauce. Stir well to combine with all the pasta.

Stir in the pine nuts and fried mushrooms and season well.

Transfer to a warmed dish and serve right away.

*TIME: Preparation takes about 10 minutes.
Cooking takes approximately 25 minutes.*

Mixed Mushroom Sauce

SERVES 4

Any variety of edible mushrooms can be used

INGREDIENTS

3 tablespoons olive oil

2 cloves garlic, finely chopped

6 ounces button mushrooms, thinly sliced

4 ounces Shiitake mushrooms, thinly sliced

2 ounces dried mushrooms, covered with
tepid water for 20 minutes

$^1/_2$ cup heavy cream

salt

1 pound fresh tagliatelle

1 tablespoon freshly chopped parsley

Heat the olive oil in a saucepan and fry the garlic until it begins to brown.

Add the sliced button and Shiitake mushrooms and fry until they darken and brown a little.

Drain the reconstituted dried mushrooms, retaining the liquid, and add them to the other mushrooms in the pan. Fry for a further minute then add 2 tablespoons of the reserved soaking water and leave briefly to reduce.

Lower the heat to a gentle simmer and add the cream. When the sauce has warmed through remove the pan from the heat.

Bring a large saucepan of lightly salted water to a boil and cook the tagliatelle for about 5 minutes, until just tender *(al dente)*. Thoroughly drain the cooked pasta in a colander.

Return the hot pasta to the saucepan and pour in the mushroom sauce. Toss to coat the tagliatelle and distribute the mushrooms.

Transfer the pasta to a warmed serving dish, garnish with the chopped parsley and serve right away.

TIME: Preparation takes about 15 minutes, plus soaking.
Cooking takes approximately 25 minutes.

Fresh Green Pesto

SERVES 4

This stunning combination of flavors goes well with any pasta

INGREDIENTS

3 ounces fresh basil leaves

3 cloves garlic, crushed

2 tablespoons pine nuts, toasted

6 tablespoons extra virgin olive oil

2 ounces freshly grated Parmesan cheese

salt and freshly ground black pepper

1 pound fresh pasta of your choice

fresh basil leaves to garnish

freshly grated Parmesan cheese, for sprinkling

▌ Pound the basil leaves, crushed garlic and toasted pine nuts to a paste, then slowly add a tablespoon of olive oil and a sprinkling of grated Parmesan at intervals until it is all incorporated and you have a smooth and creamy green paste.

If you have the time and you possess a pestle and mortar, prepare the pesto by hand – the smell is truly intoxicating. A food processor can be used if preferred.

▌ Season with a little salt and plenty of pepper and allow to stand for a couple of hours for the flavors to infuse.

▌ Cook the pasta of your choice in the usual way until just tender *(al dente)*. Just before you drain off the cooking liquid use a tablespoon of it to thin down the pesto.

▌ Drain the pasta thoroughly, transfer it to a bowl and toss it with three-quarters of the pesto. Arrange the pasta on a large serving dish and spoon over the remaining sauce.

▌ Scatter over some fresh basil leaves for garnish and serve immediately with a large bowl of fresh Parmesan cheese.

TIME: Preparation takes about 25 minutes, plus standing.

Cooking takes approximately 5 minutes.

Pappardelle with Corn & Cauliflower

SERVES 4

Using the freshest vegetables is the key to the success of this dish

INGREDIENTS

salt and freshly ground black pepper
1 pound fresh pappardelle
1 medium cauliflower, broken into walnut-size
flowerets
2 cobs of fresh corn
butter
4 tablespoons olive oil
4 ounces freshly grated Parmesan cheese
2 ounces raisins
handful of mint leaves

Bring a large saucepan of lightly salted water to a boil and cook the pappardelle for approximately 5 minutes until just tender *(al dente)*.

While the pasta is cooking half-fill another two saucepans with water, add a pinch of salt to each and bring to a boil. Place the cauliflower flowerets in one saucepan and allow them to simmer for 5 minutes.

Place the corncobs in the other saucepan and allow them to cook for just a couple of minutes. When they are ready drain the vegetables in a colander.

Run a knife several times along the length of the cob just below the surface to break off the cooked niblets, collect them in a bowl and melt a little butter over them.

Drain the cooked pappardelle thoroughly and return to the saucepan. Add the olive oil, Parmesan and plenty of seasoning and lightly toss together.

Add the cooked cauliflower, corn, raisins and a handful of mint leaves and mix with the pasta until evenly distributed.

Transfer to a warmed dish and serve immediately.

TIME: Preparation takes about 10 minutes. Cooking takes approximately 20 minutes.

Fresh & Sweet Tomato Sauce

SERVES 4

This refreshingly simple sauce tastes superb stirred into freshly cooked pasta

INGREDIENTS
1½ pounds ripe plum tomatoes
olive oil
1 medium onion, finely chopped
1 tablespoon tomato paste
1 teaspoon dried oregano
1 tablespoon clear honey
8–12 fresh basil leaves
salt and freshly ground black pepper
1 pound fresh spaghetti
extra basil leaves to garnish

▌ Using a sharp pointed knife remove the stem end from the tomatoes.

▌ Bring a large saucepan of water to a boil and drop the tomatoes in for about 20 seconds. Remove using a slotted spoon and immediately refresh under cold running water. Peel off the skins and discard.

▌ Heat 2 tablespoons of olive oil in a medium-sized saucepan and fry the chopped onion until soft and lightly browned.

▌ Roughly chop the tomato flesh and add it to the saucepan along with the tomato paste, this will deepen the color and intensify the tomato flavor.

▌ Stir in the remaining ingredients, cover and allow the sauce to simmer for 15–20 minutes. If the sauce becomes a little dry at any point during cooking add a small amount of cold water.

▌ While the sauce is simmering, bring another saucepan of water to a boil and add a little salt and a few drops of oil.

▌ Add the fresh spaghetti to the pan and simmer for about 3–5 minutes until just tender *(al dente)*. Drain the pasta and toss it in a little olive oil and freshly ground black pepper. Spread over a large serving dish.

▌ Try a little of the tomato sauce on a teaspoon and adjust the seasoning if necessary, adding a little more honey to heighten the sweet tomato flavor if you wish.

▌ Pour the finished sauce over the spaghetti and garnish with a few torn basil leaves. Serve immediately.

TIME: Preparation takes about 10 minutes. Cooking takes approximately 30 minutes.

72

Farfalle in Peanut Sauce

SERVES 4

This sauce has a glorious subtle nutty flavor

INGREDIENTS
2 tablespoons butter
2 tablespoons flour
1 1/4 cups fresh milk
1 tablespoon crunchy peanut butter
1 tablespoon clear honey
1 ounce salted peanuts, crushed
4 tablespoons heavy cream
freshly ground black pepper
1 pound fresh farfalle
fresh chopped cilantro, to garnish

▌ Melt the butter in a saucepan over a low heat, add the flour and stir together for 1 minute.
▌ Slowly begin adding the milk, a little at a time to begin with, stirring it into the sauce. Gradually increase the flow until all the milk is used and the sauce is smooth and of coating consistency.

▌ Add the peanut butter, honey and crushed peanuts. Incorporate them into the sauce using a balloon whisk. Stir in the cream and some fresh black pepper and keep the sauce warm.
▌ Bring a large saucepan of lightly salted water to a boil and cook the pasta for approximately 3 minutes until just tender *(al dente)*. Drain the pasta thoroughly in a colander.
▌ Return the cooked farfalle to its saucepan and add the peanut sauce. Toss to coat the pasta thoroughly, then transfer to a serving dish.
▌ Garnish with lots of chopped cilantro and serve hot or cold. This dish tastes equally good when allowed to cool and served as an accompaniment.

TIME: *Preparation takes about 10 minutes. Cooking takes approximately 20 minutes.*

Spaghetti with Olives & Scallions

SERVES 4–6

This simple dish can be enjoyed as a main course or as an accompaniment

INGREDIENTS
salt and freshly ground black pepper
olive oil
1 pound fresh spaghetti
1 bunch scallions, chopped into
1-inch lengths
8 ounces fresh black olives, drained
2 ounces shelled walnuts, chopped

Bring a large saucepan of salted water to a boil and add a few drops of oil to prevent the pasta from sticking. Cook the spaghetti for approximately 3–5 minutes until just tender (*al dente*).

While the pasta is cooking, heat 2 tablespoons of olive oil in a saucepan and lightly fry the chopped scallions until softened. Do not let them brown.

Add the olives and roll them around in the pan with the scallions until they are well coated in oil and warmed through.

Thoroughly drain the cooked spaghetti and tip it into a bowl. Season with plenty of salt and freshly ground pepper and add a little more olive oil.

Briefly toss the pasta before adding the scallions and olives and mixing them thoroughly with the spaghetti.

Tip the finished pasta onto a large serving plate and sprinkle over the chopped walnuts. Serve immediately.

TIME: Preparation takes about 10 minutes. Cooking takes approximately 15 minutes.

75

Index